GW00645041

The Home Edit

A Guide to Organizing Home and Conquering
the clutter with style

Margaret Trent

CONTENTS

Introduction

They don't call this book up for nothing. Whether you simply need some mess-clearing solutions before guests arrive, follow these expert-approved organizing tips to tackle clutter in every part of your home. There are hacks for spaces of varying shapes and sizes: the most-visited rooms (bedrooms, bathrooms, and kitchens), popular nooks and crannies (drawers, closets, and kitchen cabinets), and places that become the catch-all for, well, everything (desks, dresses, and shelves). The choice is yours: Declutter your entire home or pick a few organizing methods to take control of your home one small step at a time. As a result, you might even free up some extra space ... which isn't an excuse to fill it with more stuff, just sayin'.

From the kitchen and bathroom to the bedroom and laundry room, there are manyways to simplify, streamline, and banish clutter throughout the house.

It's a truth universally acknowledged: An organized home is a happy home. And not just because it's easier to find what you need. In fact, research has shown that cluttered spaces can cause more unnecessary stress than you think. You may find yourself scrambling to find keys and wallets before rushing out the door. Mornings may mean time spent searching for soccer cleats and missing socks instead of sharing breakfast as a family. Even meal prep can quickly go awry when you find yourself searching high and low for a roasting pan or container of spices you swore you still had.

With a few simple tricks and tools, you can organize everything from stacks of sweaters in the closet and piles of paperwork at your desk to baking essentials in the kitchen and spare linens in the laundry room in a few hours (or less!).

Read on for more of our pro organizing tips, sure to help you straighten out your space in no time.

Chapter 1: A 5-Step Process for Organizing Any Space

Whether you're organizing a junk drawer, a storage area, or your kitchen, the process for organizing is the same. So let's break it down...

Step 1 – EVALUATE

Start your project by determining the "mission" of the space/room. Don't skip this step. You need to determine specifically how you want this space to serve you so you'll know what things ultimately belong in that space.

Make the Decluttering Process a "No Brainer"ining Time - 0:26

Ask yourself this question:

What functions will this space serve?

Is it a multi-purpose space? For example, most of us use our kitchen for meal preparation, food storage, and eating family meals. Perhaps you also use your kitchen table as a homework station/craft area for your young kids.

If so, then it makes sense for craft supplies to be stored in the kitchen.

In my home, our guest room is a multipurpose space. Not only is it used as a bedroom, we also use it to store print photos/scrapbook albums, and gift wrap supplies.

So when I come across items that don't fit into the category of Gift Wrap Supplies, Photos, or Houseguest Items, they need to be moved out of the space during the Purge step.

Step 2 – SORT

Step 1 is all about evaluating *the space* you are organizing. In step 2, you continue to wear your "evaluation hat", but now you will be evaluating *each item* that's currently in the space.

Word of warning: this is where things get messy, so mentally prepare yourself for things to get worse before they get better!

SORTING PREP WORK

As you begin the sorting process, it's helpful to have some specific tools on hand to make the process go more smoothly. You'll need trash bags, sorting containers and some sort of signage to identify sorting categories.

I recommend creating a decluttering kit to have on hand for your organizing projects.

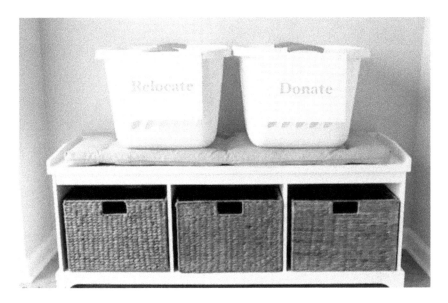

You'll need a large flat surface to sort your items. You can use a bed, large table, or kitchen island. If your space is extremely cluttered, set up a sorting area in a nearby room.

READY...SET...SORT!

Begin the sorting process by taking everything out. This gives you an opportunity to take a good hard look at the space to determine how you might improve upon it.

I recently gave this kitchen utensil drawer an overhaul, which included getting rid of the existing utensil organizer (that wasn't ideally suited for the drawer) and replacing it with drawer dividers that worked so much better for the space.

Totally clearing the space also ensures that you evaluate every single item.

Now it's time to go item by item and sort into categories.

I like to start with an initial "rough sort", which involves deciding whether an item belongs in the *Purge* pile (anything that you can immediately let go of without even thinking about it), or the *Relocate* pile (you're keeping it, but it doesn't jive with the mission of the space and must live somewhere else).

If it doesn't meet either of these criteria, then sort the item into a logical category.

For example, when I sorted through items in my utensil drawer, I had *mixing bowl scraper*, *spatula*, and *kitchen thermometer* categories. Once you have everything sorted into categories, it becomes clear where you have excess.

{Do I *really* need 7 mixing bowl scrapers?}

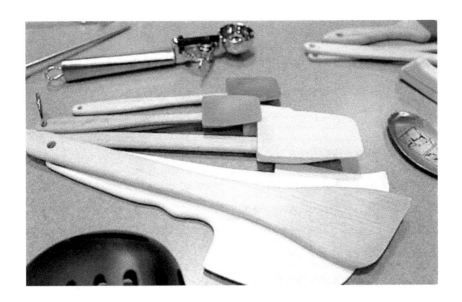

Step 3 – PURGE

O.K., ready for the tough part? If you're like most people, this step is the hardest.

It's time to make the hard decisions as to whether each item deserves to occupy precious space in your home. In my case, I had to determine if I truly needed those 7 scrapers.

Since I don't bake very often, I decided that keeping 3 was sufficient. So I picked the 3 that I like the best, bid adieu to the remaining 4 and tossed them in my *Donate* pile.

It's helpful to have a list of "Purging Prompts" as part of your decluttering tool kit. The questions that you should be asking yourself during the purging process are somewhat dependent upon the specific space you're organizing.

There are some general questions that can help you to make good decisions:

Do I love this?

When was the last time I used this?

Is this broken, worn out or past it's prime in any way?

How many of these do I have?

Is this easily replaceable?

What's the worst thing that can happen if I got rid of this?

Does keeping this align with my goal to simplify and streamline this space?

Once you've made the decision to let go of an item, you'll need to decide how it will leave your life.

WHAT TO DO WITH THE ITEMS IN THE PURGE PILE

Donate:

There are countless places that accept household donations. I'm a huge fan of donation centers that will come to your home to pick up your items.

Schedule a donation pick up as soon as possible after you complete the Purge step (or load those donations immediately in the car for drop off) to prevent the donation pile from becoming a permanent fixture in your home.

Don't forget to take advantage of the tax deduction that comes with donating household goods.

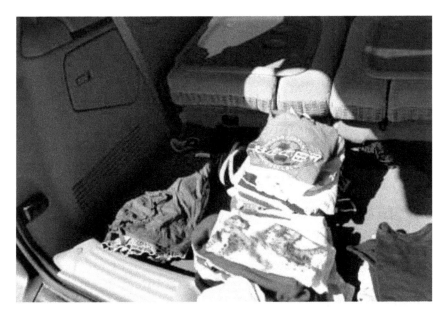

Of course, you can also donate items by giving them away to friends and family members. Just be sure to give yourself a firm deadline for delivering these items to their new home AND be sure that the intended recipient actually wants your items (many times they don't).

Sell:

Selling items in your Purge pile can make sense if you have the potential to recoup a significant chunk of change, given the time and energy required is worth it to you.

Good options for selling include: Ebay, Craigslist, consignment stores (local and online like Swap.com), and garage sales (as a last resort).

Recycle:

So many things that were once considered trash can now be recycled.

Explore the recycling resources available in your community by checking out your local waste management website (mine offers a *Recycling & Reuse Guide* that serves as a fabulous resource for figuring out where I can recycle just about anything). You can also check out Earth911.com to find recycling options in your community.

Trash:

As much as we all want to avoid contributing to the landfill, sometimes there's no avoiding it. When you come across items that are rusty, bug-infested, broken or rotten, it's simply time to trash it.

AVOID GETTING STUCK IN THE PURGE STEP

A word of caution about this step...be sure that you aren't inadvertently creating obstacles for yourself by falling prey to the idea that you can only get rid of an item if it goes to the absolute perfect home.

I've witnessed several clients getting stuck in the purge process because *"this sewing machine has to go to my sister"*, or *"I need to ship these dishes to my cousin"*. Slowly, the purge pile from one space becomes clutter that lingers in the garage or basement as these items await delivery to their final destination.

Do yourself a favor and just call Salvation Army for a pick-up. Really.

Step 4 – ORGANIZE

Finally...the fun part! In the *Organize* step, you get to assign each item a home and put systems in place for storing and retrieving your items.

Raise your hand if you've started an organizing project by going out and purchasing a bunch or pretty organizing products without a plan.

It's so easy to be seduced by all of those pretty bins, BUT if you start with this step, you've failed to get rid of the clutter first. So you'll end up organizing a bunch of things you don't use or want anymore. And that's just silly, right?

When you complete this 5-step process, you let go of the things you don't need, sort what you plan on keeping, THEN store those items in a way that works for you and your space.

Step 5 - ASSIGN A HOME

Ben Franklin said it best:

"A place for everything and everything in its place".

Sometimes the underlying problem in your disorganized space is that you've simply never assigned your items to a specific home.

Now's the time!

Follow these organizing rules of thumb as you designate homes for the items that survived the purging process:

Store an item as close as possible to where you typically use the it

Store your most frequently used items in the most accessible locations

Store item families together within zones (e.g., food prep, bakeware and clean up zones in the kitchen)

Consider safety issues (e.g., keep sharp objects and poison out of reach of the kiddos)

SUBDIVIDE THE SPACE & CORRAL YOUR CATEGORIES

At this point in the process, as yourself, "what tools can I use to best organize the categories of items I plan to store in this space?" You'll need to consider how many items you have in a category, as well as the constraints of your space.

Yey! You finally get to go container shopping! (or simply "shop your house" for items that you already have on hand).

Use products and containers to subdivide larger spaces (such as a closet or drawer) into smaller spaces.

Some examples:

{using drawer organizers to keep t-shirts organized}

{using baskets to corral scrapbooks and gift wrap supplies in a guest room closet}

{using a bakeware organizer to subdivide a lower cabinet}

{using drawer organizers to corral toiletries in the bathroom vanity}

MAXIMIZE STORAGE SPACE

Over time, professional organizers develop a bag of tricks for helping our clients maximize their storage space. Let's take a peek into that bag...

Go Vertical:

Whenever possible, "look up" and explore options for using your vertical space for storage. There are so many products that help you to go vertical...here are just a few examples:

{using a cube storage system in this client's homeschool space to store school supplies}

{using stackable bins in the pantry}

{Using clipboards and command hooks for store project papers in the home office}

Use the Ceiling:

Another often overlooked storage opportunity is your ceiling.

Using ceiling-mounted storage shelves in the garage or an over-the-island pot rack in your kitchen are shining examples of this. I've also been known to tuck seldom-used items in the rafters of my basement storage area.

Use your Doors:

Longtime blog readers are aware of my love for "back of the door" storage. It's often an untapped gold mine for beefing up storage space in your home.

{using a door rack storage system to increase pantry storage space}

{using an over-the-door shoe organizer to store office supplies}

Chapter 2: 11 Brilliant Tips to Help You Organize Your Home During Quarantine

Get the most out of your indoor time with these simple tune-ups that'll keep your house in order.

1. Get your beauty products under control.

Building a new skincare regimen usually takes a fair bit of trial and error. Unfortunately, that also means your home is likely bursting at the seams with bottles and tubes of products that you don't even use.

"Not only do new lotions, colognes, and make-up all add up over time, but they can also go bad over time," says certified professional organizer **Amy Trager**. She suggests collecting everything from your bathroom, bedroom, and wherever else they've landed, grouping like items together, and then making decisions about what you can toss. "From there, decide which categories should live where and if any containers or trays are needed to corral items coherently in drawers or on countertops," Trager says. "If it helps, you can measure your storage spaces and likely shop for containers right from home."

2. Pare down your bookshelves.

By now, we're all familiar with **Marie Kondo's** infamous "get rid of your books" philosophy. But for bookworms and avid readers, there's no way you'll ever be able to part with so many stories that still spark joy. Fortunately, a well-maintained bookshelf can actually be a great focal point for décor, if it's done right.

"If you're the proud owner of an overflowing bookshelf, then that's where reorganizing your home should start," says productivity expert and organizational coach **Linda Morgan**. "Your bookshelves can often get cluttered and messy without you really realizing it. Reorganize them into themes, color code,

24

alphabetical order, or any other arrangement that makes sense to you." It's the easiest way to bring order to some of the only visible storage space in your home. And for more storage solutions.

3. **Tackle your fridge.**

Over the course of the last few weeks, pretty much everyone has become reacquainted with cooking for themselves. And with increased kitchen production, there's even more of a need to keep things neat and tidy in your fridge. "Frankly, it's often the messiest 'cabinet' in the home," says **Orion Creamer**, CEO and founder of Big Chill appliances.

Creamer recommends installing clear plastic containers and organization bins to best utilize precious cooler space, assigning drawers or spaces to specific food categories for quick and easy access, and using masking tape and a Sharpie to label and date your leftover containers. He also suggests going through your fridge at least once a week to throw out any old or expired items. "Keeping anything that will go bad the fastest at the front should prevent any 'Oh no, this went bad two days ago!' moments," he says.

4. Clean out your cupboards and pantry.

Much like fridges can get overrun with moldy leftovers, pantries and cupboards can become a graveyard of expired spices, stale crackers, and "never gonna eat that" products. Take the time in quarantine to perform a full pantry inventory and reorganize in a way that makes things easier to find.

"If there are open items that have gone stale or aren't a part of your diet anymore, toss the food and recycle the packaging, if possible," says Trager. "Anything else you don't want should be boxed up for donation. Food pantries are still open! Do a quick online search to find one near you, call for their current quarantine hours, and drop everything off at a no-contact location."

As for the rest of it? **Jemma Lane**, interior design and marketing expert for Arbor Living Cheshire, suggests introducing jars and boxes to "help group items together and know exactly where they'll be when you need them next." That also helps you avoid accidentally buying duplicate products. And for more kitchen tips, here are the 27 Best Ways to Upgrade Your Kitchen, According to Experts.

5. Implement feng shui in your bedroom.

The ancient practice of feng shui, which revolves around the idea of harmonizing individuals with their surrounding environment, still plays a major role in interior design philosophy. And it can be an easy change to implement in quarantine, especially in your bedroom.

Try reorganizing your bedroom by putting a small night table on each side of the bed with matching lamps, says **Tsao-Lin Moy**, acupuncturist, Chinese medicine expert, and founder of Integrative Healing Arts. "This signifies there is a place for a partner and is also a feng shui cure," she explains. Moy also recommends shifting the energy of the room with a new set of matching pillowcases.

But her biggest tip is resisting the temptation to install a TV and to limit electronics as much as possible. "These are not conducive to the rest and relaxation bedrooms are meant to bring," she says. And for more tips on cutting back on screens during quarantine, check out 7 Expert-Backed Ways to Cut Back on Your Screen Time Right Now.

6. Do a room-by-room spring rearranging.

It may be a coincidence that spring cleaning time happens to fall during quarantine, but simply being at home all the time doesn't guarantee you success in your reorganization efforts. Instead of biting off more than you can chew, take things step by step—or room by room. "Choose one room each day to do a deep clean on and then open the windows and let the fresh air in," recommends **Lori Whatley**, LMFT, clinical psychologist and author of *Connected & Engaged.*

"It's also a great time to rearrange furniture and freshen up the look for spring. Just moving furniture—even just throw pillows—can help you feel less cramped and trapped during a long quarantine," she says.

Whatley also suggests using this time to repair or discard broken items in each room, as well as to "get a Mr. Clean pad and finally clean the doors, walls, and baseboards of scuffs."

7. Bring your favorite belongings to the front.

When reorganizing your home, it's important to set yourself up for continued success by making sure you come up with a good placement system. Prioritizing your items and keeping the things you use most within easy reach can be one of the best ways to keep things from getting disorganized yet again.

"Take your kitchen cupboards, for example: Ask the question 'Do I use this every day?' If so, bring it to the front, so it's most easily accessible. If not, push it to the back, or move it to the top shelves out of reach," says **Bella Middleton**, founder of Norfolk Natural Living. This same philosophy can also apply to your bedroom closet, where special garments live behind your everyday wardrobe.

This not only makes finding what you're looking for quick and easy, but it also makes cleaning up and putting things away a breeze as well. And if you need help in your kids' rooms, check out 15 Genius Design Tricks for Hiding Children's Toys.

8. Perfect your new home office.

The beginning of quarantine also marked the first time tens of millions of people began working from home for the first time in their careers. If you're one of them, reorganizing your home to include a workspace that works for you should be near the top of your priority list. "Start by asking yourself questions about how and where you like to work and observe your own habits," says **Jenny Kim**, vice president and creative director at Convene. "Figure out what works best for you at different times of day with varying tasks at hand, and shape your environment and daily routine around it."

Kim also suggests bringing plants into your space to breathe some life into your home office, choosing an area that helps you feel energized, and optimizing your desk and seating setup by using ergonomic task chairs, footstools, and computer screen height adjustments.

9. Sort through your electronics.

Think back to 10 years ago: How many electronic devices have you owned and replaced since then? The answer will likely shock you, but probably not as much as the amount of clutter they and their components can create in your home without warning. Luckily, quarantine provides the perfect cleanup opportunity to finally ditch that iPod from 2006.

"Gather all of your electronics and cords and go through them all to see which actually work and which don't," suggests **Arin Michelle Weisner**, director of client services at RedPeg. "Once you've matched all your items with their respective chargers and figured out which you want to keep, make a pile of the rest and search online for safe disposal options. Places like Staples often accept old cords and electronics for proper recycling." And for more recycling ideas you probably didn't know about, here are 23 Things You Had No Idea You Could Recycle.

10. Make your furniture movable.

Spending all of your time at home may have you using rooms you've never used before. So if your guest room/office/yoga space/meditation room is going to be filling so many roles, you might as well make it as easy as possible to move things around.

"Invest in some casters and put them on chairs, ottomans, desks, and other furniture to be able to easily roll them around when you need to create more space for an in-home workout or a conference call," says **Alicia Weaver**, chief creative officer of Alicia Weaver Design. That way, you'll never bump into your storage bench while transitioning to warrior pose ever again!

11. Get your bathroom in order.

"Many people have 'organizing bathroom drawers and cabinets' right at the bottom of their to-do list—which is unfortunate, because they're often filled with expired toothpaste, old prescriptions, spilled makeup, and worse," says Morgan.

She suggests sorting through all the products in your cabinets, drawers, linen closets, and shower area, just as you would a pantry or fridge. Then, ditch any duplicate, empty, or expired items. Another great way to cut down on shower clutter? Installing a soap, shampoo, and conditioner dispensing shower caddy.

Chapter 3: Expert Advice: 9 Tips for Creating the Illusion of Space

1. Resist the urge to go miniature.

Above: An oversized wardrobe in Geffen's former bedroom.

"Don't be afraid to place regular-sized furniture in small spaces. When you put tiny furniture in a small space, the room will actually feel smaller. I encourage you to play with scale. You can still use the negative space wisely to help the eye move throughout the room."

2. Lay out "rooms."

Above: Rugs designate an entryway (in the background) and a living area (in the foreground).

"Use rugs to designate space. This is especially helpful in studios or open floor plans. Use a large rug for your living space, and a runner to create an entry. Textiles add richness to the space while giving you creative freedom."

3. Check for visual balance.

"Rely on creative styling to offset any odd configurations. In small spaces, we often have to sacrifice ideal spacial planning in order to fit in what we need. Strategically place a plant next to your sofa that is slightly off-centered in the room, so that the eye won't notice, or place art lower than you normally would to add visual weight where needed." (Case in point: in her Echo Park apartment, Geffen couldn't find a way to center the sofa between the windows, so she added an oversized potted plant to distract the eye.)

4. Where there's a window, add a mirror.

Above: An easy way to "double" your windows. Photograph from **10 Easy Pieces: Leaning Floor Mirrors**.

"Mirrors create the illusion of bigger space. If you can, place a mirror across from a window. It will reflect the outdoors/what's outside and make your space feel larger."

5. Close a door.

"Invest in multipurpose pieces. Perhaps you can find a coffee table or bench with hidden storage inside, or a credenza with doors that will hide items you don't want seen, while still being able to place your favorite decorative items and books on top to display."

6. Add height.

Above: Efficient vertical storage, including stacking stools and a tall hutch.

"Build up. Use the wall space, as you may not have as much floor space to work with. Shelving can hold books, records, ceramics, etc. Get creative with it."

7. Fake taller windows.

Above: Illusions of grandeur: photograph from **Improper Bostonians: Jeffrey and Cheryl Katz at Home on Beacon Hill**.

"If you have drapery, hang the curtains from the ceiling, rather than from the top of the window. This will create the illusion of higher ceilings. You can also use drapery to create doorways and soften the space."

8. Make blank space intentional.

"Leave some negative space on the walls. If you have a lot of art to display, I recommend spacing the pieces out throughout the room. I don't follow 'rules' in design, but I tend to dislike gallery walls in small spaces because this can make rooms feel tight and cluttered. Place a few pieces together on one wall, and then leave the rest of the wall naked. This will allow the eye to glide through the space."

9. Take your time.

Above: Plenty of blank space—and playing with scale—in Geffen's Echo Park bedroom.

"Stay true to yourself. Don't allow lack of space to make you feel like you have to sacrifice personal style. You want your space to feel like you, as well as to serve you. Sometimes, you need to leave all of the rules at the door. Have fun with designing, and take your time in order to know how you want each area to function in order to make every square foot count."

Chapter 4: Organizing Tips for the Tidiest Home

1. Teach the "One In, One Out" Rule

Kids need to understand that storage is finite, and that continuing to collect eventually leads to clutter and chaos. When they get a new toy or new jeans, send an old one to the donation bin.

2. Hang Pots and Pans

Instead of taking up valuable cabinet space with these clunky items, use Command Hooks to hang them on an unused wall, like this pro organizer did. Start by hanging the biggest items first, then incorporate the medium-sized ones and finish with the smallest items.

3. Hang a Towel Bar Over the Sink

It looks cute (so you won't seeing it every day), and puts towels, measuring spoons, mugs or whatever else you like within easy reach.

4. Repurpose a Magazine File

Corral hot tools (once they've cooled!) on a vanity with a decorative magazine holder.

5. Use Clear Canisters

If your kitchen lacks storage, your counter will feel the brunt of the problem. So choose pretty containers (and not a lineup of grocery store boxes) when you have to devote visible space to food.

6. Do a Spin Move

A simple rotating caddy means that you'll never be caught standing over a hot stove without spoons within easy reach.

7. Hang a Hair Station

Affix small bins with adhesive strips on cabinet doors to create a home for hot tools, brushes, and hair ties. A magnetic strip keeps bobby pins, nail clippers, and tweezers from getting lost.

8. Hang Toiletries on Hooks

First, add a second tension-mounted shower curtain rod to your shower, close to the wall. Then, use hanging clips (such as "C" clip curtain rings) to hold toiletries.

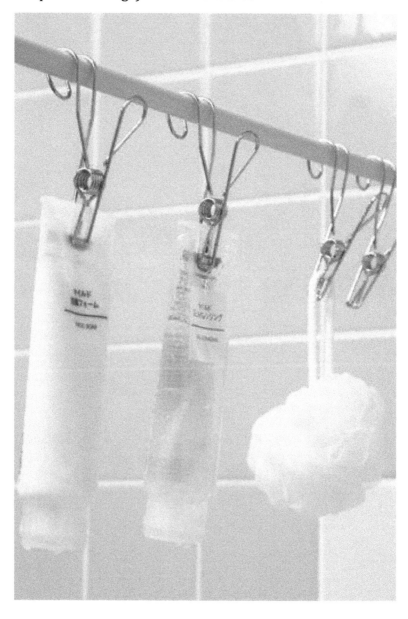

9. Use a Blanket to Contain Playtime

"When your little ones play with Legos, figurines, or other multi-piece toys, start by laying out a large blanket or bed sheet first," suggest Joy Cho, founder of *Oh Joy!*. That way, when it's time to clean up, you can bring the ends of the blanket together and quickly dump the toys back into their storage bucket.

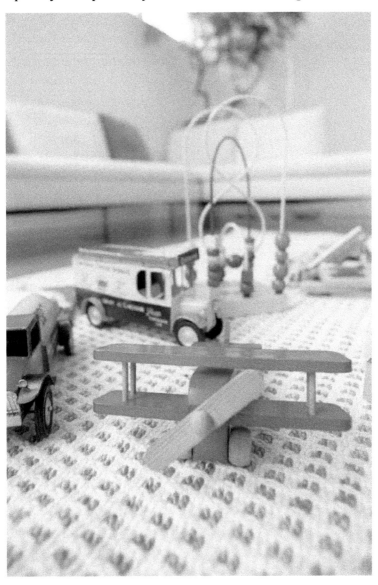

10. Pop Your Yoga Mat Below a Shelf

A yoga mat is one of those things that doesn't take up too much space yet can be awkward to store. The best bet is to hang them on the wall, like this brilliant idea that places the yoga mat in a shelf bracket.

11. Corral Underwear

Storing undies in cute compartments helps you instantly see every pair you own.

12. Store Shoes Heel to Toe

By organizing your shoes from heel to toe, you can maximize space (a.k.a. room for more shoes!), giving you a quick survey of color, toe style, and heel height to help speed up getting dressed.

13. Make Pet Food More Manageable

Instead of scooping Fido's kibble from a precariously floppy bag, minimize the chance of a big spill by pouring the food into a studier, wide-mouthed bin. This one's a spray-painted popcorn canister leftover from the holidays.

14. Reclaim Garage Ceiling Space

A utility space is perfect for hanging sturdy racks overhead.

Try this trick for storing seasonal items you don't always need to access quickly.

15. Double Up on Hangers

Hooked together with a can tab, two hangers eat up way less closet space.

Lightning Source UK Ltd.
Milton Keynes UK
UKHW021832091221
395377UK00009B/570